OF HEAVEN

GARRETT HONGO

ALFRED A. KNOPF

THIS IS A BORZOI BOOK
PUBLISHED BY ALFRED A. KNOPF, INC.

Some poems in this work were originally published in the following publications: *Bamboo
Ridge: The Hawaii Writers' Quarterly, Blackwarrior Review, Crazy Horse, Field, The Minnesota
Review, NER/BLQ: New England Review and Bread Loaf Quarterly, Ohio Review, Ploughshares,
Pequod, The Reaper, River Styx, Southwest Review, TriQuarterly, The Western Humanities
Review,* and *ZYZZYVA.*

"Ancestral Graves, Kahuku" was originally published in *The American Poetry Review,*
Volume 17, Number 1.

"Volcano House" was originally published in *Antaeus,* Number 58.

"Choir" was originally published in *The South Atlantic Quarterly,* Volume 86, Number 1,
Winter 1988. Copyright © 1988 by Duke University Press.

"The Pier" was originally published in *Chelsea.*

My gratitude to the MacDowell Colony, the Research Council of the University of
Missouri-Columbia, and the National Endowment for the Arts for assistance during
the writing of this book.

I wish to express my particular thanks to Cynthia Thiessen, Wakako Yamauchi, and Greg
Pape for their support and encouragement through the years.

Library of Congress Cataloging-in-Publication Data
Hongo, Garrett Kaoru, [date]
The river of heaven.
I. Title.
PS3558.O48R58   1988   811'.54   87-40485
ISBN 0-394-56843-5
ISBN 0-394-75785-8 (pbk.)

Manufactured in the United States of America
Published March 14, 1988
Second Printing, May 1988

The River of Heaven is the 1987
Lamont Poetry Selection of the
Academy of American Poets.

From 1954 through 1974 the Lamont
Poetry Selection supported the
publication and distribution of
twenty first books of poems. Since
1975 this distinguished award has
been given for an American poet's
second book.

Judges for 1987: *Philip Booth,
Alfred Corn,* and *Mary Oliver.*

BOOKS BY GARRETT HONGO

The River of Heaven　1988

Yellow Light　1982

THE RIVER OF HEAVEN

for June
w/ aloha
from Garrett

14 Mai '89

THE RIVER

POEMS BY

NEW YORK   1988

to the memory of my father,
Albert Kazuyoshi Hongo,
and in memory of my grandfather,
Hideo Kubota

ka poʻe o ka ʻāina me ka ʻāina

Contents

THE RIVER OF HEAVEN

Mendocino Rose

In California, north of the Golden Gate,
the vine grows almost everywhere,
    erupting out of pastureland,
from under the shade of eucalyptus
    by the side of the road,
overtaking all the ghost shacks and broken fences
    crumbling with rot
and drenched in the fresh rains.

It mimes, in its steady, cloudlike replicas,
    the shape of whatever it smothers,
a gentle greenery
    trellised up the side
of a barn or pump station
    far up the bluffs above Highway 1,
florets and blossoms,
    from the road anyway,
looking like knots and red dreadlocks,
    ephemeral and glorious,
hanging from overgrown eaves.

I'd been listening to a tape on the car stereo,
a song I'd play and rewind,
    and play again,
a ballad or a love song
    sung by my favorite tenor,
a Hawaiian man known for his poverty
    and richness of heart,
and I felt, wheeling through the vinelike curves
    of that coastal road,
sliding on the slick asphalt
    through the dips and in the S-turns,
and braking just in time,
    that it would have served as the dirge
I didn't know to sing
    when I needed to,
a song to cadence my heart
    and its tuneless stammering.

Ipo lei manu, he sang, without confusion,
  I send these garlands,
and the roses seemed everywhere around me then,
  profuse and luxurious
as the rain in its grey robes,
  undulant processionals over the land,
echoes, in snarls of extravagant color,
  of the music
and the collapsing shapes
  they seemed to triumph over.

PART ONE

. . . Shall goodwill ever be secure?
I watch the long road of the river of stars.

LI PO

Nostalgic Catalogue

for Gerald Stern

clumps of spinach gritty with sand in the seaside lot;
calabash tangle foaming in the surf,
    shaking its bracelets of hollow beads and seafluff;
black urchins bubbling in the tinned bucket,
    spikes, tentacles, needles, and dimpled shells,
    poisonous bundles decipherable to the Chinese,
    delicious to eat;
the Portuguese hiking their carnival skirts,
rolling the cuffs of their khaki pants
and wading the reef out to sea;
sour stars of green fruit in newspaper cones;
bad teeth, medicine in blue bottles, lip-paint;
78s heavy as stone hissing under the roosterhead
                of the phonograph;
soldiers on a cluttered bureau,
sepia-toned portraits splashed with fine lines of script;
Jeeps, artillery on trailers, troop carriers
              in a long caravan,
their headlights switched on, yellow through the afternoon;
Army surplus dumps, powdered cream in mud-colored tins;
Pilot crackers, canned meat, dried Chinese plum seeds
                brined in salt;
incense sticks in a sand bowl, brass temple bells,
        and black-lacquer Japanese trays;
an urn of ashes, a wooden doll
    the old folks wept over odd days;
the sizzle of rain on the highway, on the sea,
on the far approach of night traffic on its way toward town;
lipstick Buicks with white interiors
stopping roadside on Saturdays full of tourists
in sunglasses, hats, Bermuda shorts,
             and polka-dot dresses;
conch shell souvenirs, huge and pink-lipped,
    white pricetags dangling like liprings;
"76" stations with their jars of green oil,
    free pens and shirtpocket calendars
          slick as a dog's tongue;
sexy pinups, orange-fleshed and cartoonlike
on the back wall by the lube-rack;

orders from uncles and telephones full of questions,
    strange voices demanding somebody to be home;
a baby elephant in harness, pulling a wagon
          full of blue seats,
eating Pall Malls by the pack
in the dirt lot by the sugar mill;
the green milt of the *koi* pond,
the rusting screen of the cat-net that covered it,
its face-powder lilies with orange-flame hearts
    and green bedquilts of pie-pan leaves;
the swatches of color-wheel fish splashing in them,
extraordinary with Chinese names unpronounceable,
full of fortune and strange tales;
the Green Lady rocking in her aqueous cradle of weeds,
rising from the sea at night, persistent in dreams,
    in warnings, in the made-up stories of cousins who lie;
creeks full of silver and black-barred fish
that loved shrimp balled on small, golden hooks;
chilly waters and the undulant stripes of mullet
          schooled near shore;
coral cuts, the animalcula building that reef
         in your blood;
a kite, box-like, assembled in air,
holding its place in a high wind,
the sketch of an astonished face
bobbing over the temple grounds and grey tile roofs,
as old men chant unknowable tunes
and hand over the red strings.

Village: Kahuku-mura

I'm back near the plantation lands of cane and mule trails
and narrow-gauge track rusting in the rainbow distance
against the green cliffs and bridal veils of the *pali*.

I know the mill is just beyond my sight,
around the sand point, past old caneland
cleared now for prawn farms and melon patches,
and that the village is beyond them, Quonset huts
and barracks in clusters arranged without pattern.

I remember someone—Iiyama-*san*—kept a carp pond,
and·someone else made bean curd, fresh,
every day, and my chore was to fetch it,
in a bucket or a shallow pail or a lunchbox,
and I'd rush through the dusty, unpaved streets
winding past the rows of tiny shotguns,
thrilled with my job, anxious to get to
the low, barnlike building all in shadow
and cool as a cave in the middle of the day.

I'd knock or call—*Tadaima!*—as I was taught,
in Japanese for this Japanese man (other words
for the Portuguese or Chinese or Hawaiian),
and he'd slide the grey door back, *shōji*-like,
on its runner, opening up, and I'd see,
under dim lab-lights, long sinks like flumes
in three rows all brimming with a still water
lustrous and faintly green in the weak light.

There was an odor too, stark as dawnlight,
of fermentation I'd guess now, the cool paste
curdling in the damp, cold dark, silting
clear water milky under the coarse wire screens,
the air gaseous and fragrant and sharp.

It must have been a dime or a nickel—
I remember its shine and the coin's neat fit
in my hand—and he'd take it, drop it in
a slotted coffee can, then reach a slick palm,
small spade of flesh, into the supple water,

draw the raw, white cube, delicate and new,
drenched in its own strange juice, and place it,
without words or ceremony, into the blank pail
I held before me like a page to be written on.

How did I know it would all recede into nothing,
derelict shacks unpainted and overgrown
with morning glories, by canefields fringed
with *ekoa* and castor beans, swinging
their dark, brittle censers over the road?
How did I know my own joy's beginning
would be relic in my own lifetime?

I turn up the dirt road that took me in,
the green cane all around me, flush by the roadside,
a parted sea of masts and small sails scissoring the air,
whispering their sullen history on a tuneless wind.

Ancestral Graves, Kahuku

for Edward Hirsch

Driving off Kam Highway along the North Shore,
    past the sugar mill,
Rusting and silent, a haunt for crows
    and the quick mongoose,
Cattle egrets and papaya trees in the wet fields
    wheeling on their muddy gears;

We turn left, *makai* towards the sea,
    and by the old "76,"
Its orange globe a target for wind
    and the rust, and the bleeding light;
Down a chuckholed gravel road
    between state-built retirement homes
And the old village of miscellaneous shotguns
    overgrown with vines, yellow *hau* flowers,
And the lavish hearts and green embroidery of bougainvillaea
    stitching through their rotting screens.

At the golf course, built by Castle & Cooke
    by subscription, 60 some years ago,
We swing past Hole No. 7 and its dying grass
    worn by generations of the poor
And losing out to the traps and dunes
    pushing in from the sea.

It's a dirt road, finally,
    two troughs of packed earth
And a strip of bermuda all the way
    to the sandy point
Where, opposite the homely sentinels
    of three stripped and abandoned cars
Giving in to the rain and its brittle decay,
    a wire fence
Opens to the hard scrabble of a shallow beach
    and the collapsing stones
And the rotting stakes,
    o-kaimyō for the dead,
Of this plantation-tough
    cemetery-by-the-sea.

Ancestral Graves, Kahuku

We get out, and I guide you,
    as an aunt did once for me,
Over the drying tufts and patchy carpeting
    of temple moss
Yellowing in the saline earth,
    pointing out,
As few have in any recent time,
    my family graves
And the mayonnaise jars empty of flowers,
    the broken saucers
Where rice cakes and mandarins were stacked,
    the weather-smoothed
Shards of unglazed pots for sand and incense
    and their chowders of ash.

The wind slaps through our clothes
    and kicks a sand-cloud
Up to our eyes, and I remember
    to tell you
how the *tsunami* in '46 took out
    over half the gravesites,
Tore through two generations,
    most of our dead
Gone in one night, bones and tombstones
    up and down the beach,
Those left, half-in, half-out of the broken cliff
    harrowed by the sea.

I remember to say that the land,
    what's left of it,
Still belongs to the growers,
    the same as built the golf course,
Who own, even in death,
    those they did in life,
And that the sea came then
    through a vicious tenderness
Like the Buddha's, reaching
    from his lotus-seat
And ushering all the lost and incapable
    from this heaven to its source.

I read a few names—
    this one's the priest,
His fancy stone scripted with ideograms
    carved almost plain by the wind now,
And this one, Yaeko, my grandfather's sister
    who bedded down one night
In the canefields and with a Scotsman
    and was beaten to death
For the crime—
    a hoe handle they say—
Struck by her own father,
    mythic and unabsolved.

Our shame is not her love,
    whether idyll or rape
Behind the green shrouds and whispering tassels
    of sugar cane,
Nor is it the poor gruel of their daily lives
    or the infrequent
Pantomime of worship they engaged in
    odd Saturdays;
It is its effacement, the rough calligraphy
    on rotting wood
Worn smooth and illegible,
    the past
Like a name whispered in a shallow grave
    just above tideline
That speaks to us in a quiet woe
    without forgiveness
As we move off, back toward our car,
    the grim and constant
Muttering from the sea
    a cool sutra in our ears.

O-Bon: *Dance for the Dead*

I have no memories or photograph of my father
coming home from war, thin as a caneworker,
a splinter of flesh in his olive greens
and khakis and spit-shined G.I. shoes;

Or of my grandfather in his flower-print shirt,
humming his bar-tunes, tying the bandana
to his head to hold the sweat back from his face
as he bent to weed and hoe the garden that Sunday
while swarms of planes maneuvered overhead.

I have no memories of the radio that day
or the clatter of machetes in the Filipino camp,
the long wail of news from over the mountains,
or the glimmerings and sheaths of fear in the village.

I have no story to tell about lacquer shrines
or filial ashes, about a small brass bell,
and incense smoldering in jade bowls, about the silvered,
black face of Miroku gleaming with detachment,
anthurium crowns in the stoneware vase
the hearts and wheels of fire behind her.

And though I've mapped and studied the strike march
from the North Shore to town in 1921, though I've
sung psalms at festival and dipped the bamboo cup
in the stone bowl on the Day of the Dead,
though I've pitched coins and took my turn
at the *taiko* drum, and folded paper fortunes
and strung them on the graveyard's *hala* tree;

Though I've made a life and raised my house
oceans east of my birth, though I've craned
my neck and cocked my ear for the sound of flute
and *shamisen* jangling its tune of woe—

The music nonetheless echoes in its slotted box,
the cold sea chafes the land and swirls over gravestones,
and wind sighs its passionless song through ironwood trees.

More than memory or the image of the slant of grey rain
pounding the thatch coats and peaked hats
of townsmen racing across the blond arch of a bridge,
more than the past and its aches and brocade
of tales and ritual, its dry mouth of repetition,

I want the cold stone in my hand to pound the earth,
I want the splash of cool or steaming water to wash my feet,
I want the dead beside me when I dance, to help me
flesh the notes of my song, to tell me it's all right.

Pinoy *at the Coming World**
Waialua Plantation, 1919

I thought, when I left the fields
and hauling cane and hoeing out the furrows
for this job of counting and writing and palaver
in the rough, sing-song English of the store,
I had it made and could scheme a little,
put away something, so long as I made
the balance at the end of the day
and nobody squawked to the bosses
that I cheated or sassed them.
And I shamed no one, reading the paper
or some cowboy dime-novel like a *haole*
showing off my literacy as they shuffled into the store
dressed in their grimed khakis,
cuff and gloves sticky with juice,
and nettled head to toe with cane fiber.
I could speak Ilocano like a king or a muleteer,
a Visayan pidgin, a Portuguese,
a Chinese, and a Puerto Rican.
Simple words for service.
But for jokes, for talk story,
we used the English—chop suey at first—
then, year by year, even better,
smooth as love between old partners.
And the insults—*bayow, salabit, bagoong!*—
no matter if affectionate or joshing,
never entered my speech again
from the day I left the ditches,
tied on the apron, and stepped behind this counter.
No more *"manong,"* no more "rat-eater" or "fish-brain."
No more garbage-talk to anybody.
How I see it, we all pull a load,
glory across the same river.
So, when I brought the wife in and the babies
start to coming—American citizens every one,
born, not smuggled here—I had every reason to figure,
"Pinoy, no worry, you going to the top."

*The poem depends, in part, upon an oral history available in *Hanahana: An Oral History Anthology of Hawaii's Working People*, compiled by the Oral History Project of the University of Hawaii at Manoa.

Even when the strike came and the black market
started to cut me out, I wasn't surprised.
The union had told me to stay on,
keep open even though they picketed.
When they needed cigarettes, sugar, or coffee,
when they needed box matches to light
torches at the labor rally,
they still came to me, calling from the back door,
and I sold in secret, out of pity,
and, for the plantation, at a profit.
Nobody lost. And I had the goodwill,
fish or vegetables or papayas whenever anyone had extra.
They came to the back, just as during the strike,
handing things through the door in old rice sacks
and smiling, bowing if they were Japanese,
and running off down the street past the Cook pines
without much to say, bowing each time they glanced back,
framed in the green monkey-tails of the trees.

But none of us was ready for the flu that hit,
first the Mainland and all the reports of dead
on newspapers wrapped around the canned meats I stocked—
drawings of mourners joining hands in long processions
following a single cow draped in white,
a black parade on an unholy day—
then here at Pearl by cargo and troop ship,
through the military and workers at the docks,
finally to all of us here on the plantations,
diggers and *lunas* and storekeepers all alike,
sick with it, some of us writhing on the beaches,
sleeping naked and in the running wash from the waves,
shivering, trying to cool our fevers down.

My boys were worse with it at first,
all of them groaning like diseased cattle,
helpless and open-eyed through the night.
But they slipped the worst punch
and came back strong, eating soup
and fruits and putting the weight back on.

17

The oldest even went back to school
and took over for us behind the counter
times when my wife left to nurse the sick
and I boarded the stage for Honolulu,
hoping to fetch medicines from the wholesalers
and maybe a vaccine from the doctors at Pearl.

But it's my youngest now that has it bad,
so weak in years English is her only tongue,
fevers all the time and a mask of sweat
always on her face. It's worse because
she doesn't groan or call out or say anything much,
only coughs and rasps in her breathing
like a dull saw cutting through rotten wood.
We pray, bathe her face and neck and arms
in a cheesecloth soaked in witch hazel,
light a few candles, and call on the saints
to cure her and to ease our pain.

But I know it's near her time
and that no faith doctor or traveling *hilot*,
our village healers expert in herbs and massage,
will bring her back from this final sickness.

Last night, when waiting was all there was to do,
I dressed myself in khakis again
and a pair of work boots so new
the laces were still full of wax
and soles like iron against the soft heels of my feet.
I closed up and walked past
the mill and the raw sugar bins,
by the union hall used for a morgue
and past the locomotive bedded down for the night.
I wanted to walk completely off plantation grounds
and get all the way out of town to where
sugar cane can't grow and no moon or stars
rose over pineapple fields. I wanted to get up
on a ridge someplace where kings
and their holy men might have sacrificed
or buried, in secret, some intruder's
unholy bones. I wanted rain to fall
and streams to churn and waterfalls, as they fell
from the *pali* across mossy stone, to glow

with the homely, yellow light of mourning, our candles
lit for the souls unwinding in their shrouds
and shrieking off the cliff-coasts of these islands.
I wanted the roar from the sea, from falling water,
and from the wind over mounds and stones
to be the echo of my own grief, keening within,
making pure my heart for the world I know is to come.

IN MEMORY OF SILME DOMINGO

Jigoku: *On the Glamour of Self-Hate*

I must have always wanted to go it alone
ever since I left Hilo that morning
on the troop ship bound for Korea
and the skirmishes and hordes of dead
and taunts rising from the bunkers,
from scattered members of our island platoon
announcing they were still alive.
I remember walking, stumbling over sandbags
and the half-corpses of dead G.I.s;
and, at the end, there were only three of us—
me, the medic, using a rifle for a crutch,
and the other two hanging on to me like crabs
grabbing at the head and tail of the bait.
We made jokes, called each other *sissy* and *slopehead,*
but, inside my bones, I hated them
for whining and calling on the Buddha,
and I walked out alone, scavenging from the dead,
counting cadence to an old work song.

After that, I was in Japan, evacuated,
hanging around the ward,
loitering in the barracks and the PX
before they chased me and I mustered out.
I came home and stuck around there too,
doing nothing much but sleep and gamble whenever I could,
dressing up in starched khaki slacks and an orchid shirt
I found one day in a Schofield thrift store.
When my brother sent bonds home,
bought with his overseas pay,
I cashed them quick as they came in
to pay off my debts or else put new bets down
at the chickenfights or fan-tan joints on Hotel Street.
I figured he had it easy—guard duty in Germany
while I was being shot at, patching the wounded.
When I won, I'd pay him back, but meanwhile,
I filled my life with the splendor of gestures
and gamblers' calls, putting my swag down,
snaking my arm around a pool-cue in a basement hall
or a slim whore in a Suzi Wong at a ticket dance.

I got a name—Flash—to fit my quickness and my style,
and began to affect the Macao fashion
of ice-cream suits, white Panama, and saddle shoes.
If collectors got offended, I never knew it
and could saunter through Chinatown on Mauna Kea Street,
whistling and jingling change in my pockets,
picking plumeria, a rose or dyed carnation
from the lei stands for my wide lapel—
no one knocked my hat off or spit across my shoes.

After a while, I got a reputation agreeable to me
as one with connections, who knew the moves
of the roulette wheel at the Royal Hawaiian
before H.P.D. could shut it down,
who scheduled the payment sacks
between mah-jongg parlors and opium dens,
the interest rates and favorite *maiko-san*
of the *yakuza*, the virgin geishas raised like orchids
in the moist gardens behind the laundries.

But it was all a fiction—I swaggered and was ignored
because I lost continuously and kept the *bobora*,
the foreign Japanese with crew cuts and Hong Kong suits,
entertained with my flamboyant dress and unsolicitous banter.
I teased them and wheedled them and stroked their cash
like a younger sister encouraging their larger bets,
and swaddled them in the jasmined arms of the women
who began to follow and to court me, stripped of their sex,
sensing I, numbed with pride, was stripped of mine.

We all made money—me, the whores, and the *yakuza*—
and, while I kept mine circulating, I never
lost out completely, but shaved my debtors
and put something into a girl of my own,
a *ha-pa* kid, half white, half Japanese,
ai-no-ko we say, child of love,
who showed up one day behind the counter
at the Kokusai movie house.
I asked her if she liked to dance, and we went—
foxtrot and tango and jitterbugging—
until she was mine and I,
despite the crimson and green dragons
and black-scaled clown fish

Jigoku: *On the Glamour of Self-Hate*

tattooed over my shoulders and back,
pledged myself to freeing her from the lotus-world
we called *Jigoku,* Kingdom of Earth.

She wanted to act and to sing, and to wear,
like the *femmes* whose make-up sketches
she studied from *Vogue* and *Look* and *Photoplay,*
that pitiable menagerie of doll's clothes
from the chintz shops and pattern stores
that flirted, simply, in a swirl of cloth.
She studied fabrics and perfumes
and a repertoire of permanent waves,
practiced ways of walking to entice and a sneer
to return us all to short pants and our mothers' laps.
I paid for tap and ballroom dance lessons
and a bogus charm school advertised as Barbizon.
Yet, I sensed she could do it,
more than voluptuousness under that ice-cream skin
I kissed by the faucet in our six-dollar room
as she stooped, nude over the porcelain basin,
at night or in the morning or in the middle of the day.

She waitressed cocktails at Waikiki and the Crouching Lion,
wore *muumuus* and sarongs and made her tips
from the tourists and the off-duty military.

I thought of the torch ginger the whole time,
a waxen lotus petalled in flames, large as a fist,
spectacular, without fragrance or fragility.

Nights alone, back in the hotel, I laid my bets down
calling from the pay phone down the hall,
trying not to hear the hoots and the whistles
from the colored Johns as they stepped from buses,
the bars and the cabs, lining up for the midnight parade.

One morning, after another solitary night
listening to the small gangs of petty crooks
thrashing below my window like a caustic tide
thick with the miscellany of wreckage,
I took off for Japan without waiting to say goodbye,
but leaving a note, written in the blockish,
unrefined script that always shamed me,

recommending her to the Chinaman's care, Wo Fat,
his restaurants, his brothels, and private string of girls.

Over there, I caught on to a Catholic school,
taught their girls English and started turning grey,
letting my flesh get soft and my style disappear.
I wore gabardines, oxfords, orlon sweaters
and corduroy coats patched at the elbows,
began haunting *pachinko* parlors
in Ebisu and Gotanda at night—the cheap streets
where *takarazuka* nude shows were about a buck,
the beer fifty cents, and the girls to be had
for whatever nothing your loins could pay.
I won laundry soap, rice crackers and gimlet water,
metal-wrappaed packets of seaweed and cough drops,
and condoms in a vacuum tin;
and I hunkered down in a gorgeous anonymity,
consoling my flesh with magazines
already blued by the censors
and cutting loose the past to drift, guiltless,
on the aspic of Tokyo's squalid, human sea.

In my rooming house, back in the six-mat room
over the dry-goods store, I listened
to Nat Cole 78s on the scratchy hi-fi
and sometimes thought ahead, years in the future,
to meeting death one day, a cousin or a nephew
I've never known who'd recognize me
browsing in the oldies section
of a stateside record store.
He'd see the family sadness
in the loose flesh of my jowls,
the unembittered shame in the way
I slouched over album bins
and tried to imagine myself full of exultation,
rapt as I gathered and stacked,
in the crook of my arm, those machine-spun
rituals of tenderness called the blues.
He'd address me in a schooled Japanese
and I would deny him *and* myself,
fake a country tone to my speech
and pray he'd miss the unforgivable hang of my clothes,

a drapery without tradition except in our islands,
clinging, even then, to my isolation and my resolve.

Days later, in a press room, at a terminal
typing out his lead or a finish on deadline,
his face like the raw page decorated
in a green calligraphy of light emanating
from the screen, he might think back
to our meeting among the brutal currents
of idlers in the shopping mall and imagine me,
discovered, finally, by some fishermen,
sliced from my clothes and under six fathoms
in the boat channel of Hilo Bay,
fused in a posture of supplication
and folded, as a fan is folded,
tucked to fit the trunk of my car,
tattoos at last flailed from my skin,
and, cut away from bone, the white threads of flesh
a gossamer I pass through from this world to the next.

Hilo: First Night Back

There are things tonight I've never known:
Aunt Lily's face like my father's, the glance
from a squealing child that seems my own,
a way of speech with echoes all the way
to the everlasting. My father's people like gifts
arranged around me for the first time;
and the last time 30 inarticulate years ago—
some infant bawling in blue blankets,
my mother's arms wrapped around him
like a coat of warm wind.

                    Revelations tonight:
my lost family of artists and entrepreneurs,
Aunt Charlotte's anthuriums and baby's breath
in twists of modish *ikebana* on the television,
and Bobby, my father's younger brother, is still far away,
the stories about him mounting,
cloned mysteries prolific in imagination.
We write our name this way,
as I suspected, with flourishes,
and my grandmother's still alive
teaching *odori* in Honolulu.

                    What's the news
of this world? The volcano I was born under?
All I had of my father's past a paling photograph,
small as a half-dollar
whirling in my memory. He stands in front of
the old store, dressed in a T-shirt and loose cotton pants,
skinny as DiMaggio and in dark glasses,
holding the baby squirming in his arms
to face the camera, sunlight and time
in cascades of white from the borders
erasing us year by year.

Hilo: First Night Back

                              Proud to be back
under the navy wool of this night sky,
the angle Orion takes from here
to everywhere I've been. Silver giants slice
these heavens. A small crane
tumbles in its long flight home.

Eruption: Pu'u O'o

We woke near midnight,
flicking on the coat closet's bulb,
the rainforest chilled with mist,
a yellow swirl of gas
in the spill of light outside.
Stars paling, tucked high
in the sky's blue jade,
we saw, through the back windows
and tops of *ohia* trees,
silhouettes and red showers
as if from Blake's fires,
magenta and billows of black volleying.
Then, a burbling underground,
like rice steaming in the pot,
shook through chandeliers of fern
and the A-frame's tambourine floor,
stirring the cats and chickens
from the crawl-space and their furled sleep.
The fountain rose to 900 feet that night,
without us near it, smoking white,
spitting from the cone 6 miles away,
a geyser of flame, pyramids and gyres of ash.
Novices, we dressed and drove out,
first to the crater rim, Uwekahuna
a canyon and sea of ash and moonstone,
the hardened, grey back of Leviathan
steaming and venting, dormant under cloud-cover.
And then next down Volcano Road past the villages
to Hirano Store on Kilauea's long plateau.
There, over canefield and the hardened lava land,
all we saw was in each other's eyes—
the mind's fear and the heart's delight,
running us this way and that.

Crossing Ka'ū Desert

from under the harpstring shade of tree ferns
and the blue trumpets of morning glories
    beside the slick road,
the green creep of davallia and club moss
    (their tiny hammers
            staffed quarter-notes
    and fiddlenecks on the forest floor),
spider lilies and ginger flowers like paper cranes
    furling in the tongues of overgrowth,
        in the sapphired arpeggios of rain

to the frozen, shale-colored sea,
    froth, swirls, bleak dithyrambs of glass,
a blizzard of cinderrock and singed amulets,
warty spires and pipelines,
    threnodies of surf whirling on the lava land—

our blue car the last note of color
driving a black channel
        through hymnless ground

Cloud-Catch

He must have come wanting little,
  except to belong to the land,
red volcanic soil loamed with ferns,
  drenched in mists and the constant drizzle
of 4,000 feet and the cloud-catch of Mauna Loa,
  amphitheater for rain and sunshowers,
and to his own father as well,
  a cab-driver who'd run off,
leaving him, boy of 6, with an aged nurse
  and friend-of-the-family
after his own wife—was it arranged?—
  a picture bride
from Kumamoto supposed to be *odori-ko*,
  a dancer-apprentice,
had run off too, out of shame or boredom,
  or to flee his brutality.
Who can say? So long ago, and the times were such
  people changed names, even countries,
easily as writing them differently,
  a few dollars for the document—
"Bear-Haven" or "Fukui-ken"
  for Hawaii, Kingdom of Heaven—
or else stealing off in the foreign night
  as if beating a debt
without a sentimental glance
  back to the village they'd left,
shacks and rice paddies, a pile of gravestones,
  or to the schooner that brought them,
or the husband and infant
  they might have abandoned.

After 19 years, a stint at war, raised up
  shining shoes on Nuuanu,
he was, I'm sure, ready to belong to anything,
  even to this father
who had called for him
  on his last chance,
ill and certain of being dwindled
  to the nothing

spreading from his bones through his failing body.
   It was a final deceit,
another ruse to get service and advantage—
   a suitor or salesman smiling at the door,
doffing his straw hat, the bouquet of roses
   or aluminum assortment of spoons
cradled in a sleeved elbow—a kind of absolution
   while he lingered,
hovering yet in this life,
   extracting its last gift,
my own father there, at bedside,
   stroking his hair,
holding or not holding the living hand,
   swindled again.

Don't look back, he'd say,
   making a G.I.'s joke back home in L.A.,
grinning from over the sports page after dinner,
   the TV on with its silly din
of quiz shows and Mom on the phone
   or washing dishes,
my brother out in the summer yard
   pitching a tent by the apricot tree.
And that's about all I do,
   piecing the lives together,
getting the stories folks will tell me,
   dust in the gleam of light
swirled with a cupped hand,
   finding a few words.
They're not enough, though,
   no matter how sweet or bitter,
the purple sails of clouds here like outriggers
   steering home to their island,
and, curse or song, I know nothing much stays,
   that even love drips,
tear by drop, quenching barren ground.

Volcano House

for Charles Wright

Mists in the lantern ferns,
    green wings furled against the cold,
and a mountain wind
    starts its low moan through *ohia* trees.
The lava land blazes in primrose and thimbleberry,
scented fires of pink and blue
    racing through jungled underbrush.
I'm out feeding chickens,
    slopping a garbage of melon seeds and rind
over the broken stones and woodrot of the forest path.
I'm humming a blues,
    some old song about China Nights
and boarding a junk,
    taking me from my village.
Miles in the distance,
    Kilauea steams and vents
        through its sulphurous roads,
and a yellow light spills through
    a faultline in the clouds,
glazing the slick beaks of the feeding chickens,
    shining in their eyes
like the phosphorous glow
    from a cave tunneled miles through the earth.
What was my face before I was born?
    the white mask and black teeth
at the bottom of the pond? What is the mind's insensible,
    the gateless gate?
Through overgrowth and the leaning drizzle,
through the pile and dump of tree fern
    and the indigoed snare of lasiandra
shedding its collars of sadness by the broken fence,
I make my way down a narrow path
    to the absolute and the house of my last days,
a dazzle of light scripting in the leaves and on the weeds,
    tremors in the shivering trees.

The Unreal Dwelling: My Years in Volcano

What I did, I won't excuse, except
to say it was a way to change,
the way new flows add to the land,
making things new, clearing the garden.
I left two sons, a wife behind—
and does it matter? The sons grew,
became their own kinds of men,
lost in the swirl of robes, cries
behind a screen of mist and fire
I drew between us, gambles I lost
and walked away from like any bad job.
I drove a cab and didn't care,
let the wife run off too, her combs
loose in some shopkeeper's bed.
When hope blazed up in my heart for the fresh start,
I took my daughters with me to keep house,
order my living as I was taught and came to expect.
They swept up, cooked, arranged flowers,
practiced tea and *buyō*, the classical dance.
I knew how because I could read and ordered books,
let all movements be disciplined and objects arranged
by an idea of order, the precise sequence of images
which conjure up the abstract I might call
yūgen, or Mystery, *chikara* . . . Power.
The principles were in the swordmanship
I practiced, in the package of loans
and small thefts I'd managed since coming here.
I could count, keep books, speak English
as well as any white, and I had false papers
recommending me, celebrating the fiction
of my long tenure with Hata Shōten of Honolulu.
And my luck was they bothered to check
only those I'd bribed or made love to.
Charm was my collateral, a willingness to move
and live on the frontier my strongest selling point.
So they staked me, a small-time hustler
good with cars, odds, and women,
and I tossed some boards together,
dug ponds and a cesspool,

figured water needed tanks, pipes,
and guttering on the eaves
to catch the light-falling rain,
and I had it—a store and house out-back
carved out of rainforests and lava land
beside this mountain road seven leagues from Hilo.
I never worried they'd come this far—
the banks, courts, and police—
mists and sulphur clouds from the crater
drenching the land, washing clean my tracks,
bleaching my spotted skin the pallor of long-time residents.
I regularized my life and raised my girls,
put in gas pumps out front, stocked varieties of goods
and took in local fruit, flowers on consignment.
And I had liquor—plum wine and *saké*
from Japan, whiskey from Tennessee—
which meant I kept a pistol as well.
My girls learned to shoot, and would have
only no one bothered to test us.
It was known I'd shot cats and wild pigs
from across the road rummaging through garbage.
I never thought of my boys,
or of women too much until my oldest bloomed,
suddenly, vanda-like, from spike
to scented flower almost overnight.
Young men in model A's came up from town.
One even bussed, and a Marine from Georgia
stole a Jeep to try taking her
to the coast, or, more simply,
down a mountain road for the night.
The Shore Patrol found him.
And I got married again, to a country girl
from Kona who answered my ad.
I approved of her because,
though she was rough-spoken and squat-legged,
and, I discovered, her hair
slightly red in the groin,
she could carry 50-lb. sacks of California Rose
without strain or grunting.
As postmaster and Territorial official,
I married us myself, sent announcements
and champagne in medicine vials
to the villagers and my "guarantors" in town.

The toasts tasted of vitamin B and cough syrup.
My oldest moved away, herself married
to a dapper Okinawan who sold Oldsmobiles
and had the leisure to play golf on weekends.
I heard from my boy then, my oldest son,
back from the war and writing to us,
curious, formal, and not a little proud
he'd done his part. What impressed me
was his script—florid but under control,
penmanship like pipers at the tideline
lifting and settling on the sand-colored paper.
He wrote first from Europe, then New York,
finally from Honolulu. He'd fought,
mustered out near the Madison Square Garden
in time to see LaMotta smash the pretty one,
and then came home to a girl he'd met in night school.
He said he won out over a cop because he danced better,
knew from the service how to show up in a tie,
bring flowers and silk in nice wrappings.
I flew the Island Clipper to the wedding,
the first time I'd seen the boy in twenty years,
gave him a hundred cash and a wink
since the girl was pretty,
told him to buy, not rent his suits,
and came home the next day, hung over,
a raw ache in my throat.
I sobered up, but the ache
stayed and doctors tell me
it's this sickness they can't get rid of,
pain all through my blood and nerve cells.
I cough too much, can't smoke or drink
or tend to things. Mornings, I roll
myself off the damp bed, wrap
a blanket on, slip into the wooden clogs,
and take a walk around my pond and gardens.
On this half-acre, calla lilies in bloom,
cream-white cups swollen with milk,
heavy on their stems and rocking in the slight wind,
cranes coming to rest on the wet, coppery soil.
The lotuses ride, tiny flamingoes, sapphired
pavilions buoyed on their green keels on the pond.
My fish follow me, snorting to be fed,
gold flashes and streaks of color

like blood satin and brocade in the algaed waters.
And when the sky empties of its many lights,
I see the quarter moon, horned junk,
sailing over Ka'ū and the crater rim.
This is the River of Heaven. . . .
Before I cross, I know I must bow down,
call to my oldest son, say what I must
to bring him, and all the past, back to me.

PART TWO

I can negate everything of that part of me that lives on vague nostalgias, except this desire for unity, this longing to solve, this need for clarity and cohesion. I can refute everything in this world surrounding me that offends or enraptures me, except this chaos, this sovereign chance and this divine equivalence which springs from anarchy.

ALBERT CAMUS

Morro Rock

for Mark Jarman

—a Thirties blue fedora
slouching through thick China fog off the Pacific;
or, in bright sun, the grey colt
romping in curls of surf, the wash
at its heels, foam breaking against the slate chest;
Duchamp-Villon's horse stolen from its museum
and spray-painted camouflage green
sliding from the junker pickup
speeding along Highway 1, bouncing from its crate
as it slams across asphalt and the gravel shoulder,
at rest, finally, in the cold sand,
nose awash in running tide,
some huge and abandoned engine
stripped from its hot car,
salvage in the sea's green oil,
churning still in the vicious pistons of surf.

I remember best stories in which it figures
as centerpiece or sublime backdrop:
the great albacore run of the Sixties,
men in fraying mackinaws stained with blood
crammed thick as D-Day on the decks
of an excursion or half-day boat
chugging slowly through light fog,
slicks belowdecks, poles high-masted,
a small denuded forest on the sea's false winter,
maybe a thousand fish iced in the hold,
the coast in sight, harbor invisible
except for the black bead of the Rock,
a notched landfall, eloquent on the horizon.

Or the time I played Weston with it,
forcing my father to drive north one day,
up the coast through patchy fog to the Bay.
We stopped at an overlook
snarling with brush and bunches of iceplant,
and he chose the shot, setting the tripod,
while I fiddled with filmpacks
and tested the cloth shutter in the car.

Morro Rock

We waited an hour for the fog to be right—
the Rock emerging from it, finally,
a black clipper from the sea.

And I knew a girl once
who lived near there,
and whom I'd visit,
hitching north, needing her still.
She was the first I'd known
who could sit, oblivious,
still in her long shift,
pull both knees to her arms,
and rock gently in the sand
while a thin film of sea washed around her.
I'd stand barefoot in the foam
while the ocean percolated around us,
and toss wet handfuls of sand
towards the combers, empty of feeling.
The Rock filled the space behind us.

Sometimes though,
it's successful lovers I recall,
the battered myth of my teens,
a cheap tale told over bonfires
snapping with kelp and whistling driftwood.
They were young too,
or old beyond counting,
a bachelor Abraham and maidenly Sarah
working their poor farms
on opposite ends of the cove.

They saw each other Sundays at church,
sold raffle tickets and donated specialties
to the annual charity auction—
he volunteered lessons in pier fishing,
she, a picnic lunch in the park by the dunes.
Shyly at first, then with humor and verve,
they bid for each other, waving off competitors.
There was a season of courtship—
football games, holiday dinners together,
a New Year's Eve with foreign champagne
and Glenn Miller records on the hi-fi.
By the next spring, they were making love,

discreetly at first, then, finding the gods
in each other, fierce as teenagers
parked by the Rock, they'd kiss openly,
sprawl over each other on blankets at the Esplanade,
ignoring first the whispers, then the minister's call
and letters of petition from the neighbors.
Before the police could come,
after indecent afternoons under the pier,
riders in pickups came,
hooded like hanged men or cowled in ski masks.
There were women too, undisguised
in their housedresses but keening in the night
as they assembled, crowlike, by the farmshack.
No gunfire, the lovers were killed with stones,
with the snapped limbs of beach oak
and a quick, purging fire of hate.

Before death, smeared with bruises
and the beach tar and twigs of ritual,
the couple spoke through their wounds
and fear of death, mumbling an exchange
of pledges and a curse for the Bay.

The following day, the charcoaled pillars
and collapsed floor still hissing,
a pair of cranes landed, loonlike,
from the overcast, snow-flurried skies.
A runaway chill spreading south from the Sierras
had brought them, and the steaming ruins
made their haven from the cold.
They danced a curious rite of celebration,
blue and grey-tipped wings furling,
red dandelion crests erect,
lifting from ground to air like curling smoke,
until, finally, by early evening,
they drifted downwind past the town
and landed cloudlike, small white floats,
plumed gardenias on the Rock's dark brow.

Love is always violent *and* sacred, and though death
might be peace, dying often seems love's own act,
a strong taking and the murder of reason.

Morro Rock

All is true, a story sanded by several tellings
until it shines, jewel in the soft fingers of tide,
the constellated image high in its heaven of likenesses.

It doesn't matter how I think of it,
it continues to define itself,
this chunk of continent equal to nothing.

Metered Onramp

There's a swale of new fieldgrass,
rainsprung, green against the sandy brown
of a long rise of vacant land
sloping under power lines
that pursues me through sleep
and waking daydream wherever I've been.
It's beside the freeway,
by the Alondra onramp,
a patch of wild land full of blown garbage,
a motley of torn newspaper and tin cans
piled against one of the tower struts.
Sometimes I'd see boys playing with sticks
around the tower legs, dodging in
and out of skeletal shadows at sunset.
And at night, or twilight,
we commuters crouching in exhaustion
at our steering wheels,
I'd see the bums and the ragpickers,
the shopping bag people
with their makeshift rakes
and scavenged hand trowels,
sifting through the loose dirt and refuse piles
for whatever treasure they could find—
maybe cigarette butts, maybe deposit bottles
still intact, maybe flecks of shiny metal
or the rare bauble of an heirloom trinket
some crow may have snatched off your bureau
one night with all away at the movies—
something. I'd see them bending in the tall grass
like campesinos stooped over lettuce fields,
bobbing in the blond summer rye
like cricket pumps working an underground pool,
or, in late winter, sloshing through the mud
and fresh revivals of grass after a thorough rain,
dressed in castoff trenchcoats, dingy
and ripped somewhere at the sleeve,
exposing the layers of stinking flannel
and polyester sprouting from the tear.
What were they really after? Something

precious, I might guess, something
without value for us but essential to them
as credit or the lustrous and fragrant
heat of the body after sex. I could
make something up, or I could try
to remember what one of them told me once—
that all the numbers, Arab and Chinese, were buried
just below the topsoil, that they slept
seedlike in the earth waiting for the rains,
the right and warm ones of spring,
and needed to be stirred from their loamy beds,
alerted to their task of keeping track of the world.
Her name was Sally, I think,
and she reeked of wine and excrement
but always had money, wadded up
like pads of Kleenex mixed with carrot tops
and cabbage leaves stuffed in the deep pockets
of her long Joseph's coat.
Once, in the early morning of another smoggy day,
the ground fog tendrilous through the purple weeds
and ghostly wireworks of the tower,
I saw her near the top of the long slope,
poised as if to begin a fast downhill.
She was in a crouch, knees coiled
and shoulders hunched, dressed
in rummaged lime-green slacks, layered T-shirts,
and the salvaged coat of many colors.
She stood up for an instant,
waved at us as we waited in the onramp's cue-line,
maybe signalling she was ready.
Car horns went off,
and I could hear some carpoolers
squealing at Sally's grand ridiculousness
as the light went green. She crouched again,
then launched herself, bellyflopping
in the grass and the mud, rolling
over and careening down the slope
like a downed racer spilled from his skis.
She seemed to stop more than a couple of times,
blocked by a tire or a trough in the dirt,
splashing in puddles,
but kept going, shoving herself downhill,
flinging her body shoulders first

44

and scuffling over the crusts of mud
and small piles of broken fencing.
All the while she flailed her arms,
billowing her open coat that,
now drenched in fresh doses of mud,
slapped and whispered sexually
against her spindly thighs.
Hallelujah, she was saying,
A-le-leu, over and over
as we marvelled, crouching in our cars.

The Sound of Water

At the No. 1 Café, waiting for his lunch
of boiled noodles and sliced fishcake,
the thirtyish man smoking his Chesterfields
down to the filters is sorting through his worries,
thinking about the deductible on his dental coverage,
and deciding, for the moment, that he might
sacrifice an aching molar to the impassive
gods of industry and conspicuous consumption.
Floor mats, he sighs, blowing smoke like a bad valve,
Brand-name shoes, his chant against the Fifties
and the marketing techniques of Sears, Roebuck.
He rubs chin-stubble with the back of his hand,
hitches his unbelted work jeans, and gazes
through smoke-blued light at the picture calendar
lightly flapping above the booth opposite his own.

He sees himself as a priest of distinction
strolling the swept grounds of the Golden Pavilion,
glossing a sutra passage on the benevolence of Shakyamuni,
composing a lecture on the Dharma
and adjusting his robes as he ducks under
the green curtain of the willow tree
rustling its prayer-beads in the wind.

The screen door bangs in the back by the kitchen,
the cook's iron spatula rings on the griddle,
and he could be the enormous, flag-spotted carp
hovering in the green murk of the lily pond
surrounding the temple, where the priest,
inattentive for once, stumbles in his wooden shoes,
losing his footing on the rock-bridge, tumbling,
sleeve-spinnakered arms reaching out for balance,
elaborate robes full of wind, sidelong into algaed
lotus waters, glimpsing the mixed clown-colors
and dull, gownlike swirl of white fins and tail
the moment before a face not unlike his own
rises through pond-scum and ten thousand years
to deliver him its wordless message
in the cold slap of his hands against flat water.

Lunch arrives, steaming in its porcelain bowl,
another culture-bound composition in splashes
of green and pink and glutinous white, brown morsels
of pork arranged rocklike in the small pond of broth.

What is it now that matters, that rules the mind?
Not the thin layer of grease and cigarette ash
on the green Formica counter, not the Platters
crooning from the tremulous juke-box, and not
the concrete grey or sprouting tatters of his T-shirt.
Money is nothing, his bills and labor are nothing,
and the heat outside, over a hundred in the shade
for the third straight day, is nothing.

There is only the vague, listless hum of an electric fan
as it lashes and purrs like an exhausted bird
trapped in the rusting wire of its cage,
and the small babble of voices talking and making orders
as customers enter and leave with a jingle of change,
and, before him, brimming in its spoon of red dragons,
the passionless sound of water—undulant, concentric—
lapping its way from a mindless center to the bone-white rim.

A Far Galaxy

for Greg Pape

Across the vacant lot and its small garden
of bean plants and corn, up on the second floor
of the stuccoed apartment house, a woman
in a blue housecoat and Hawaiian print dress
hums a medley of spirituals and TV themes,
finishing the morning dishes. She dries her hands,
wiping them on the sleeves and shoulders of her coat.
Below, between the apartment and the ivied fence
at the lot's straight edge, a gang of school kids
is playing Star Wars, shooting off mimed finger guns,
imaginary beams of red and green laserlight
zipping through the gray Los Angeles air.

One boy, dissatisfied with the limits of imagination,
considers a move beyond the naive *as if,* beyond
the repertoire of vocal effects and make-believe explosions.
He runs from his friends huddled under the whitewashed
meter box and jumps over a row of juniper bushes,
crossing the property line to the garden lot,
and weaves his way through rows of corn plants
and ripening beans. He reaches the garden hose
and grabs hold of the nozzle. On, it spits
and struggles in his grip as he aims an arching
bridge of stars over rowed cornstalks and the elfin,
ear-shaped leaves of bean plants bouncing lightly
like marionettes in the wind. Stars dust down
on his friends as they run for cover behind dumpsters
and laugh, skidding in the fresh mire by the fence.

The woman, suddenly aware of her child's voice
rising louder than the rest choiring below,
leans out over her dishrack and peeks from behind
her curtains. She yanks off her housecoat, smoothing
her dress as she tramps down, still in houseslippers,
the two flights of metal stairs to the street.

When she yells, it's like a siren and all the kids
scatter, dispersed through familiar dimensions,
running home or down the corner to regroup,

T-shirts drenched, feet shoed with mud, the good,
gray light of reason still a far galaxy, grave
and irrelevant, trapped in nebulae swirling invisibly
in the noon summer sky. A scarf of mist, iridescent
in the hot city air, shimmers through downtown smog.

The Cadence of Silk

When I lived in Seattle, I loved watching
the Sonics play basketball; something
about that array of trained and energetic
bodies set in motion to attack a more
sluggish, less physically intelligent opponent
appealed to me, taught me about cadence
and play, the offguard breaking free
before the rebound, "releasing," as is said
in the parlance of the game, getting to
the center's downcourt pass and streaking
to the basket for a scoopshot layup
off the glass, all in rhythm, all in
perfect declensions of action, smooth
and strenuous as Gorgiasian rhetoric.
I was hooked on the undulant ballet
of the pattern offense, on the set play
back-door under the basket, and, at times,
even on the auctioneer's pace and elocution
of the play-by-play man. Now I watch
the Lakers, having returned to Los Angeles
some years ago, love them even more than
the Seattle team, long since broken up and aging.
The Lakers are incomparable, numerous
options for any situation, their players
the league's quickest, most intelligent,
and, it is my opinion, frankly, the most *cool.*
Few bruisers, they are sleek as arctic seals,
especially the small forward
as he dodges through the key, away from
the ball, rubbing off his man on the screen,
setting for his shot. Then, slick as spit,
comes the ball from the point guard,
and my man goes up, cradling the ball
in his right hand like a waiter balancing
a tray piled with champagne in stemmed glasses,
cocking his arm and bringing the ball
back behind his ear, pumping, letting fly then
as he jumps, popcorn-like, in the corner,
while the ball, launched, slung dextrously

with a slight backspin, slashes through
the basket's silk net with a small,
sonorous splash of completion.

"96 Tears"

In high school, I was in a special group,
the "AP" classes, advanced placement,
segregated from the rest of the student body.
In them were mostly Japanese kids,
a few whites, and a black or two—
there were never any Chicanos—and
that was when the idea of hierarchies,
categories, and "rank" was finally made clear
to me. It's certain I'd noticed, thought
about it before—in Hawaii, when I was a child,
there were always those of us who could speak,
write, a proper kind of English (we were
always favored) and those who had only
the pidgin. I remember a boy I was trying
to help write a composition. The teacher,
Mrs. Yamamoto, had assigned me to him
as a kind of tutor (I would have been
humiliated had it happened to me), and I
was reading over his work, dismayed that it
was written in pencil rather than ink,
huddling over his shoulder, my hand on his back
like an umpire's on a catcher's, following along
as he read it aloud to me. "Spelling first,"
I said. "We check dah spelling," my own propriety
sensing this occasion as a scene for pidgin,
a discretionary moment of logocentrism
amidst this scene of discipline and *écriture.*
". . . and went the bird *ladat,*" he read,
flatly, without the risk of emphasis.
"What?" I said, suddenly puzzled.
"And den the bird *ladat* went?"
he asked, tentatively, feeling corrected,
changing his story as a suspect does
when leaned on by a cop or D.A. *Interrogated.*
"What's *ladat?*" I asked again. "You know,"
he answered, suddenly confident, relieved
that I had probably only misheard him,
that it wasn't grammar or the esoteric
subtleties of idiomatic, Mainland syntax
I was questioning. "*Ladat!* I went hit

dah bird *ladat! Ladat* I hit dah ball
wit dah bat *ladat!"* he said, popping
his fists together, chopping down, rolling
his wrists in sweet imitation of a crisp,
Aaronish swing. "Ladat," I said. "Yeah."

So, by high school, on the Mainland,
I'd already internalized
the principles of difference between the dim
and the quick, counted myself pridefully
among the sullen elite, and, jive as I was,
carried armfuls of books wherever I went
in order to show it. It was my identity,
an added sign that, I felt, cast me
tropologically free from the anonymity of other,
drifting signifiers as they swaggered
by the lockers, making time with chicks,
jingling lunch money, scuffling their feet
in a cruiser's walk so the steel taps
on their shoes would click and scrape,
rhythmically, on the pavement.
They wore their shirts open,
dark wool Pendletons in winter,
loud satins, loose and pajamalike
in the hot weather, lustrous as fishbelly,
exposing a thin jersey undershirt,
sexual, strangely cummerbundish
in its subculture formality, the rules of its wear,
and Christophers, gaudy crucifixes, or later,
and black and red leather *mo-jo* pouches
dangling like *mamori* from their necks,
signifying, testifying, and talking trash.
They were a lateral dance of signifieds,
transcendental, Temptations-like,
free and unoppressed as they walked.

"Free, white, and twenty-one" is the formulaic.
Cynical and exclusive, it doesn't mean
"Emancipation," that freedman's word,
signifying unlimited potential, an open road
like Whitman saw, a view from the prospect
of *Democratic Vistas,* a sense of magnificence
and of election.

I had two friends in school,
one Jewish, one Japanese, both very bright,
who became presidents of our student body.
They wanted the recognition
and the experience of it, I suppose,
the status and familiarity with leadership,
both as a role for themselves and as an access
to power, its rules and disdainful possessors.
We all wanted to get out.

Our school was
three thousand, urban, poor and middle class
intermingled, bordered by two freeways,
a drainage channel and corridor for power lines
with their monstrous platoons of buzzing towers
approaching campus through yellow smog.
Their lines emerged through the inland distance,
across marshlands thick with cricket pumps
and the junkyards along Figueroa.
They receded west down Artesia
over the derelict rails and crossties of the Santa Fe
down to Redondo steamplant and the invisible sea.
I won't forget the drive-in on the east side.
Singular then, it's now a multiple,
four screens mounted like newly risen moons
over the zebraed asphalt and speaker trees
of four separate lots. Adventure movies,
Disney features, and screwball comedies,
puerile sixties Day and Hudson sex romps then,
now they show soft-core porn sometimes,
white and ethnic ladies in polyester negligees
cuddling with some biker or shoe salesman
on the large rectangles stuttering with images
just visible through the stands of the football field.
On Fridays, when the spectators cheer,
sometimes it's for a good play or touchdown,
others it could be for an on-screen, comedic feel.

Not to say in my time things were nobler,
more dignified. They were not. We went
a long way for a bad joke: Steve Hamada
carved out a compartment for his portable radio
in the dense pages of the ham-sized,

Dictionary of Philosophy I think it was,
so he could tune in on KGFJ, "The Soul of L.A.,"
letting the organ-preachy strains of *96 Tears*
or some other Top 40s hit of the day
filter through the chem lab as we titrated,
90-lb. girls giggling under decorously curved hands,
we boys feigning cool, staring into the wretched paisley
of an Erlenmeyer flask full of dark precipitate,
while our short, pastry-haired teacher
(he used Wildroot, a lanoline saturate)
in his sharkskin suit bellowed threats
down the lab aisles, policing his way past
burbling tubes and long glass stir-sticks
tinkering like feeble tongues
in the pale froth of the beakers;

or the time Higashi brought in the deck
of Tijuana playing cards to sophomore gym.
I remember one card in particular,
of rose-colored and cloud-purple genitals,
a blank look of humiliation or boredom
on the aging woman's face
(the Queen of Hearts or of Spades, unmitred),
rills of fat deliquescent along her belly,
her legs parted, knees up, the dark beard
undisguised and fibrous, frank as malice
or the desires of industry, her eyes unglazed,
looking straight into the camera lens
minus the obliged and sham ecstasy
on the faces of others in the deck.
I remember my own face then, hot with puzzlement,
abashed at my own craving, exchanging
that deep glance with the nameless woman's eyes.

There are none of us elect. Jap or Sheenie
hawking rags in the New York streets,
nothing matters under corrosive skies,
the burdened light that bears down on us
with the tremulous weight of guilt and outrage.

Portrait of a Lady

Sheathed in a lucent, sky-blue Spandex suit, she reclines
on her right side on the import-store rattan mat, her back
seething with oil and the metallic sheen of pricey,
unenameled cookware. Her legs bounce in lazy, parallel waves
to the bassline of the rock tune blasting from the FM-
stereo in her screened-in porch and over the shining jasmine bush
electric with scent and the delirious, nectared hum of bees.
Once in a while, to a soul ballad or bossa nova on the charts,
she twitches her freckled shoulders, shimmies a little,
and pops the fizzing vent on a sweating can of diet cola.
It's another weekday on the front lawns and concrete driveways,
TV-time for the neighborhood's aged, PTA for amiable mothers,
alcohol and free-base for the rock-and-roll unemployed.
She suns herself because she's none of these, has leisure and a B.A.,
part-time work as a pool-typist or script girl for the movies.
She's waiting for a deal, some new idea or fresh start—
a party to go to, a car to shop for, the new boy at acting school
to ask her to Vegas or Mazatlán, for her old man to stash enough away
from his straight job for the down on their pleasure sloop
and sail them both to Tahiti—far, unpopulous Topanga—
to the opium lands and spicy archipelagoes of the South China Sea.
Her hope is for time to accelerate, for the music, amplified cadenzas
of heavy metal booming through the dry-wall of her stuccoed house,
to pick up speed, swing into exotic, too-hip rhythms,
vamping through syncopations, ritards, slight accelerando changes
to gain improvisatory verve and finesse, easing down, finally,
on the proven sweetness of an old, melodic piece of Ellingtonia.
She'd like for the asphalt streets to quake and to tear open,
preemptively, like the chasmed earth in a Fifties disaster picture,
swallow her down so she'd never again have to suffer
the anxious freedom of choosing what paper to subscribe to,
what political party, color dress or brand of eye-shadow to buy.
Cars cruise, sprinklers twist and hiss alive through the neighborhood,
and dandelions of Sierran waters sprout from parkways
and the greening lawns all around her. A cool, turgid surf
settles under her shoulders as she rolls to her back,
sighing under the lambent, vaguely effectual spray.

Four Chinatown Figures

In a back alley, on the cracked pavement slick with the strewn waste
of cooking oil and rotting cabbages, two lovers stroll arm in arm,
the woman in furs and a white lamé dress with matching pumps,
her escort in a tux casually worn—the black tie undone,
the double-breasted, brushed-velvet coat unbuttoned.
They're a Wilshire lawyer and city planner out on the town.
When they pass the familiar curio of the wishing well
with its Eight Immortals spouting aqueous wisdoms
through their copper mouths and baggy sleeves, they spend a minute
considering the impotent, green nozzle of its fountain.
The reflecting pool, speckled blue willow or streaked turquoise
as a robin's egg from the small litter of coins wintering on its bottom,
catches starlight and red neon in a tarn of winged ephemera
streaking across the black glaze of homely water. The lawyer
kisses his date and tosses some bus change, balls up
the foil wrapper from an after-dinner mint and throws that,
while she laughs, shaking her head back so the small,
mousse-stingered whips on the ringlets of her hair shudder
and dress sequins flash under the sore, yellow light of streetlamps.
Two dishwashers step from the back door of the Golden Eagle
arguing about pay, about hours, about trading green cards
with cousins for sex, set-ups with white women, for cigarettes
or a heated hotel room to sleep in on a dry, newspaper bed.
Bok-guai, they curse with their eyes, *Lo-fahn*, as the four nearly collide,
separate galaxies equal in surprise as they wheel to face each other.
The lawyer thinks little of these punks in T-shirts and Hong Kong jeans,
but the woman rhapsodizes, for no reason, in suspense/thriller prose—
slender and boylike, the bull's ring curl to their flimsy moustaches;
they must be cold in this dry, winter chill of late December in L.A.—
the sky a high velvet, indigo-to-black as it vaults, lazily,
from the city's fluorescent glow to the far azimuth
where the bear and huntsman drift casually into nothing.
Without jackets, the Chinese have bundled themselves in castoff,
cotton aprons stained with intricate patterns of lard and duck's blood
and wrapped like double-slings around their shoulders and folded arms.
Something grins on the face of the taller, fairer-complected one,
glints from his foxteeth, smolders in breathfog, camphor about to flare.
She tells herself, *Forget it, c'mon*, and, with a hooked finger,
snaps at the man's satin cummerbund. They turn away.

Four Chinatown Figures

Without a gesture, in the greasy dark, the two Chonks turn away too,
back towards each other, and hear, quickening away behind them,
steps receding into the light din of street noise and sidewalk chatter.
The fair one says, audibly and in English, *Kiss me, white ghost,*
and, briefly staggered in the amniotic burst of light
from a passing tourist's flash, shrugs off his gruesome apron,
pulling out a pack of Gauloises, blue-wrappered, *especial,*
and strikes a match, holding it in the orange well of his hands
as, dragonlike, they both light up and puff, posed on a street vent,
hunching their thin shoulders and turning uptown against the wind.

Choir

for Philip Levine

I flung back the whitewashed, garagelike door
of the ghetto church, and a sudden blast of heat,
bred in the stinking, summer dark, slavered past me
like some huge Great Dane released from its pen,
breaking free and running up the car-cramped street.
Inside, through cracks in rough shingling overhead,
through the gaps between clapboard walls and naked studs,
small filaments of light snuck back in,
settling on neat rows of metal chairs and wooden ones
scratched with use, their shiny paint chipped and peeling.
I stepped in, looked left and looked right
to the frayed bunting and army blankets and bedsheets
hanging halfway down each wall—to block out the light?
the dust? the cold in winter?—I couldn't solve it
and sighted on the small dais up front,
the preacher's podium a stamp-book card table
draped with purple velvet as if it were
the counter of a Shriner's booth at the fair.
I imagined the preacher, a large black man
robed in satin of a lighter blue, marching in ahead of the choir,
themselves gowned in blue, judge and jury to the sinning flock.
I saw him step up to the flimsy pulpit,
lean into his sermon, and open up a huge Bible
big as a drum or accordion and bound in white leather,
its garlands cascading from his surpliced belly to the dusty floor.
Well, well and *Amen* sang out, gracenotes from the congregation,
shouts and hollers for the Lord, the preacher's big voice
booming over all of theirs against the plywood walls,
his feet stomping hard on an unpainted bandstand.
I walked up the aisle past the rows of vacant chairs,
scuffling my shoes on the slick concrete,
and tried to do my job, following directions—
Go Left Behind Altar—to the square meter box beside the small shrine
thick with a forest of unlit candles for Kennedy and for Dr. King.
A huge Coptic cross presided over this, ornate and spangled,
catching fibers of light in its rhinestones and sequins
and sending them back around in fluted patterns
filigreeing everywhere, fading in the spill of light from the street.
I opened the box and read the meter's spinning dials,

recalled the legend of the dentist, supposed to be black,
who drilled a tiny hole in the glass casing
of the unit at the rear of his office,
and syringed, carefully, through a long steel needle,
a solution of sugar and powdered egg onto the flywheel
so a colony of ants could take up residence
and thus slow the register of his consumption,
bringing down his bill, saving a little for liquor
and a weekend trip to Vegas with his Oriental nurse.
We make up myths for what we don't know,
ways to excuse our own failure to turn from
ignorance and our own cruelty. In junior high,
I used to sing mornings outside the locked classroom
with a black kid, a white one, and another Japanese.
We had our own quartet and rehearsed gospel and pops,
Freedom Train, Sweet Chariot, and, I remember,
our black leader taught us the backup to *Summertime*
while he soloed, his baritone gliding to falsetto,
bouncing off the gray lockers and the blue fire doors,
spilling through the chain-link fence that kept us in
to the river of coastal fog rushing up the numbered, public street.
Together our voices made a sound none could make alone,
"Harmonics," Harold said, a tone from the choir itself,
a *pure* sound *begat* from sound, that naive exchange,
voices singing for nothing, waiting for the bell to ring.
I left the church and locked up, shielding my eyes
against the summer glare. I went away past bungalows
through the dry, sauna heat of summertime in L.A.,
witchy perfumes, gnats and mayflies, the patter of frying oil
and TV soaps and quiz shows clouding the dumpster shade around me,
ache of smog in my chest, the bramble of phone and power lines
                              seething up ahead.

The Pier

In winter, those first mornings after my father died,
I'd get out of the apartment and take walks
along the boardwalk while the wind scuffed
over low dunes on the deserted beach
and skipped trash through alleyways
I walked through on my way to the pier.
Coastal fog would sometimes shroud everything—
the few motels, small cottages miscellaneous in design,
the Bauhaus beachshack absurd with its concrete stilts
and assortment of cutout windows and color panels
like a make-up tray styled by Mondrian—
as if some gray ghost of a manta or skate
had, overnight, chosen this beachtown as its bottom
and settled, wraithlike, over all its weather and dilapidation.
Or, it would have stormed for days,
or a storm would be on its way, the pioneer
or remnant clouds like huge purple swans
gliding across the channel from Catalina
over the choppy aquamarine to the inland plains,
trailing their small skirts of rain and glory
past buzzing power lines flexing in the strong, on-shore wind.
Up on the pier, by the glassed-in lifeguard station,
I'd see couples in ski parkas and peacoats clenched against
                                                    each other
while a few gulls hovered overhead, hoarding the wind,
screeching their mild complaints. I'd see fishermen
waddle by burdened with plastic buckets filled with bait
or their poor catch of leopard sharks and Spanish mackerel,
the black, swordlike bracts and blossoms of their tails
drooping like loose bunches of glutinous flowers over the rims.
I had no heart, I felt nothing, could think
only that I didn't believe he'd died
so close to making it through—retirement
just around the two-year corner like a beacon
cutting through the gray present, the best moments
of our friendship, silent as the burst of yellow light
like a brushfire catching in all the windows
up the far, west-facing shore at sunset,
still ahead for us, loomings riding under cloud-cover,

a rosy blaze reaching out to small crafts at sea.
I'd see Vietnamese in small, family groups,
or they were Cambodians—Asians as foreign to me
as my grandfathers might have been
to the Yank seaman who stared, stopped
in his climb up the worn rigging of his tall ship,
as they tramped in wooden clogs off the *City of Tokio*
and down the "China Bridge," a long, wooden plank,
over marshy land to the Immigration Station
at Honolulu Bay. They'd be mothering handlines over the railing,
jigging a "Christmas tree" of small, feathered hooks
to catch the baitfish they'd need for the mackerel,
bonito, and flounder cruising the musseled pilings
in the green waters frothing under the pier.
For splendor, for his cheap fun, my father
would go to the track, lose himself in the crowd
milling around the paddock, weighing the odds
against the look of the horse, handicapping,
exchanging tips, rushing the window just before post-time
and rising to his feet for the stretch run,
beating cadence and whipping a gabardine pants leg
in rhythm and chant to the jockey's ride.
I think splendor must be something of what we all want
somehow, respite from privation and a world
of diminishment, a small drama so strange
it exiles the common yet thrills us with our own stories:
the mother, having lost her child, who sees,
through reeds on the riverbank, a glimpse
of the boy her child might have become,
and then herself is swept away in the river's next flooding;
the drunk who constructs, in a series of baroque fantasies,
the fabulous mansion with its Moroccan pool
surrounded by wrought-iron gates and fences, magnificently Byzantine,
while he lives out his life on the edge of a junkyard
by the drive-in, in the hulk of an abandoned automobile;
or, the poor painter who steps out from behind a woodpile
after chapel one day to denounce his younger brother,
himself a master of religious painting,
accusing him of pride and falsity, destroying his brother's faith,
gaining a small advantage and the impermanent rise of his own
reputation;
or, my favorite, the young voluptuary, frigid in her marriage bed,
who flees on a winter's night through barren woods,

escaping her peasant husband, the village, and this life,
stripping nude at riverside and plunging in,
beginning an alabaster, fetal crawl through the roiling
                                        green waters
collapsing in mock pleasure around her as she drowns,
engulfed by the image of a rising moon
breaking up and coming together again
on the slick, mutable surface of the water.
My father believed in what he could imagine for himself—
a set of numbers written like calligraphy on a handicap sheet
that translated into his occasional but regular movements
through a world made beautiful by his own need
for that beauty and its sequence of splendid events,
desire that metamorphosed into scenario after scenario
and their ritual demarcations—swans gliding
on the infield pond while a trumpet blared its call—
while that other world went on with its load of pain,
its twelvescore of humiliations and ridicule.
These immigrants, on workdays, line a certain street
up in Costa Mesa on the bluff, stationing themselves
like whores at a busstop, while cars cruise by,
suburban wagons and Euro-sedans, housewives at the wheel,
picking and choosing their day-domestics
from the lineup of illegals and boat people
begging for work, grinning at each electric window
as cars drive up, stop, and a matron leans out,
negotiates a price, opening a back door
and waving them in, or else demurs, passing all of them by,
gliding along in her polished, nearly perfect world.

The Underworld

Under the cone of flurried light
blued with cigarette smoke,
we sat in the false, morphined shade
of L.A.'s old Orpheum,
a once lavish Fox now gone to skinflicks,
horror fests and community matinees,
laughing at the silliness on-screen—
two comics, a black and a Jew,
both Afroed and dressed in chicken outfits,
trying to rob a suburban bank.
The black housewives around us
laughed too, nursing and cooing
at their infants who bawled
during the lulls and gunfight scenes,
shushing their older ones
who jounced in their seats, miming
the robot-dance or tossing popcorn, bored.
A few rows up from us was a stagpile
of the unemployed, bachelors in their twenties,
middle-aged fathers graying in cigar smoke,
all of them dressed in satins and polyesters
softly gleaming in the spill-light from the screen.
There was one in particular—a ghetto blade
in green velours—he wore a purple hat too,
and its feather, a peacock's unblinking eye,
bounced and darted, faintly luminous in the dark.
He cackled through the escape and arrest scenes,
calling out to his partners
phrases I couldn't quite make out,
then laughing and muttering deep *Yeahs*
in the rhythm of the talking around him.
I suppose they shared a thrill of recognition,
that old slap five and *I heard that*
from the street corner session,
but something passed among them,
a common pain or delight in, just once,
another's humiliation. It was Monday
or Thursday, and though no rain
was coming down in the streets

outside that I could see,
everybody seemed nonetheless well.
My friend talked about the opulence around us—
coal-black interior walls frescoed
with a chain of demons intertwined,
the stalled parade of aisle and exit lamps
(red grottoes, archipelagoes of colored light)
and plush chairs with their flower-carved fabric
and scalloped backs, the gabled balcony overhead—
everything so ornate and particularized,
designed on a theme of descent
into an irretrievable world—
summer afternoons of phosphates and cowboy serials,
or love made more than potential,
corporeal on-screen, a starlet's hair
undone and almost in your lap, *so real*
that the soul stirred in the body
like a river of cold light sliding
through a forest petrified in winter.

When we left, shuffling out behind
the small crowd lighting up their Kools,
almost embarrassed to be seen
in the harsh house lights, everyone went quiet
from the dissonance of our being there.

We stepped outside to the chill blast
of the low desert turning to fall,
city buses hissing and squeaking by,
slurs of Spanish and disco and rap,
a cop's traffic whistle, a street vendor's call,
the day's last, feeble light
streaked in the eyes, fuzzy Giotto halos
like the stiff, polyester hats
on the shimmering, mingled throngs of the poor.

The Legend

In Chicago, it is snowing softly
and a man has just done his wash for the week.
He steps into the twilight of early evening,
carrying a wrinkled shopping bag
full of neatly folded clothes,
and, for a moment, enjoys
the feel of warm laundry and crinkled paper,
flannellike against his gloveless hands.
There's a Rembrandt glow on his face,
a triangle of orange in the hollow of his cheek
as a last flash of sunset
blazes the storefronts and lit windows of the street.

He is Asian, Thai or Vietnamese,
and very skinny, dressed as one of the poor
in rumpled suit pants and a plaid mackinaw,
dingy and too large.
He negotiates the slick of ice
on the sidewalk by his car,
opens the Fairlane's back door,
leans to place the laundry in,
and turns, for an instant,
toward the flurry of footsteps
and cries of pedestrians
as a boy—that's all he was—
backs from the corner package store
shooting a pistol, firing it,
once, at the dumbfounded man
who falls forward,
grabbing at his chest.

A few sounds escape from his mouth,
a babbling no one understands
as people surround him
bewildered at his speech.
The noises he makes are nothing to them.
The boy has gone, lost
in the light array of foot traffic
dappling the snow with fresh prints.

Tonight, I read about Descartes'
grand courage to doubt everything
except his own miraculous existence
and I feel so distinct
from the wounded man lying on the concrete
I am ashamed.

Let the night sky cover him as he dies.
Let the weaver girl cross the bridge of heaven
and take up his cold hands.

IN MEMORY OF JAY KASHIWAMURA

A NOTE ABOUT THE AUTHOR

Garrett Hongo was born in Volcano, Hawaii and grew up on the North Shore of Oahu and, later, in Los Angeles. He attended Pomona College, graduating with honors, and then spent a year touring Japan and writing poetry. He did graduate work in Japanese language and literature at the University of Michigan and in English and Critical Theory at the University of California, Irvine, from which he received the M.F.A.

He published his first book of poems, *Yellow Light*, in 1982; many of the poems from that book and the present one were originally published in such magazines as *Antaeus*, *The New Yorker*, *The Nation*, *The American Poetry Review* and *Ploughshares*.

He has taught poetry at the University of Southern California, the University of California at Irvine, and the University of Missouri at Columbia, where he is Assistant Professor of English and a poetry editor of *The Missouri Review*. He is married to Cynthia Thiessen, a violinist and musicologist, and they have two children, Alexander and Hudson.

A NOTE ON THE TYPE

The text of this book was composed in a digitized version of Palatino, a type face designed by the noted German typographer Hermann Zapf. Named after Giovanbattista Palatino, a writing master of Renaissance Italy, Palatino was the first of Zapf's type faces to be introduced in America. The first designs for the face were made in 1948, and the fonts for the complete face were issued between 1950 and 1952. Like all Zapf-designed type faces, Palatino is beautifully balanced and exceedingly readable.

Composition by Graphic Composition, Inc., Athens, Georgia
Printed and bound by Halliday Lithographers, West Hanover,
Massachusetts
Designed by Harry Ford